FANTASTIC SPORT FACTS

MOTOR SPORTS

Michael Hurley

Raintree is an imprint of Capstone Global Library Limited, a company incorporated in England and Wales having its registered office at 7 Pilgrim Street, London, EC4V 6LB – Registered company number: 6695582

www.raintreepublishers.co.uk
myorders@raintreepublishers.co.uk

Text © Capstone Global Library Limited 2013
First published in hardback in 2013
First published in paperback in 2014
The moral rights of the proprietor have been asserted.

Edited by Catherine Veitch, Sian Smith, and John-Paul Wilkins
Designed by Richard Parker
Picture research by Ruth Blair
Originated by Capstone Global Library Ltd
Printed and bound in China

ISBN 978 1 406 25348 1 (hardback)
16 15 14 13 12
10 9 8 7 6 5 4 3 2 1

ISBN 978 1 406 25354 2 (paperback)
17 16 15 14 13
10 9 8 7 6 5 4 3 2 1

British Library Cataloguing in Publication Data
Hurley, Michael.
Motor sports. -- (Fantastic sport facts)
796.7-dc23
A full catalogue record for this book is available from the British Library.

Acknowledgements
We would like to thank the following for permission to reproduce photographs: Corbis pp. 7 (© Leo Mason), 9 (© Schlegelmilch), 12 (© Clifford White), 16 (© Rainer Ehrhardt/ZUMA Press), 18 (© George Tiedemann), 24 (© PCN), 25 (© Melchert Harry/dpa), 27 (© Robert Sullivan /Reuters); Getty Images p. 5 (Karl Johaentges); Photoshot pp. 6 (© Icon SMI), 10 (© Imagebrokers), 11 (© UPPA), 19 (© Talking Sport), 20, 21, 23 (© Picture Alliance), 26 (© Everett Collection); © Photoshot p. 17; Shutterstock pp. 4 (© Natursports), 8 (© AHMAD FAIZAL YAHYA), 11 (© Richard Peterson), 13 kangaroo (© Eric Isselée), 13 stop sign (© Luca Villanova), 14 (© cjmac), 15 (© CHEN WS), 21 (© Nataliia Natykach), 22 (© Studio 1a Photography).

Cover photograph of Sebastian Vettel reproduced with permission of Corbis (© SRDJAN SUKI/epa), and a car wheel reproduced with permission of Shutterstock (© risteski goce).

Every effort has been made to contact copyright holders of any material reproduced in this book. Any omissions will be rectified in subsequent printings if notice is given to the publisher.

Contents

Some words are printed in bold, **like this**. You can find out what they mean by looking in the glossary.

Motor sports basics

Motor sports are very popular all over the world. They are exciting, fast, and dangerous.

DID YOU KNOW?

The most popular motor sports include **Formula 1**, **NASCAR**, **IndyCar**, **World Rally**, and **MotoGP**.

The Nurburgring race **circuit** in Germany was opened in 1927. It is one of the longest in the world.

The fastest

The fastest vehicles used in motor sport are **drag racing** cars. They have a top speed of 531 kilometres (330 miles) per hour.

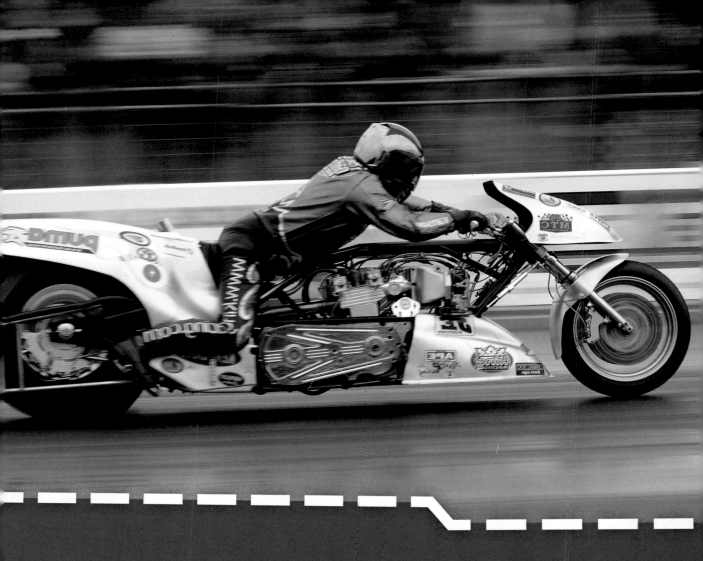

DID YOU KNOW?

The fastest bikes are also drag racers. They have a top speed of 395 kilometres (245 miles) per hour.

Getting ahead

In motor sport, gaining an edge over others can mean the difference between winning and losing.

rear wing

The huge rear wing on this car helps to keep it steady at high speeds.

extra wheel

DID YOU KNOW?

In the 1970s, **Tyrrell** developed a racer with six wheels. This amazing car won the 1976 Swedish Grand Prix.

Unusual racers

If a vehicle has got an engine, you can race it! One of the most exciting motor sports is truck racing.

DID YOU KNOW?

Racing trucks have to weigh at least 5,500 kilograms. That's the same as a bull elephant!

You can race lawn mowers, too! Racers improve their mowers so that they **accelerate** more quickly.

WHAT WILL PEOPLE BE RACING NEXT?!

Kangaroo stops race!

In 2007, during the famous Bathurst 1000 race in Australia, a kangaroo appeared and bounced around on the racetrack! Incredibly, no one was injured, and the kangaroo escaped unhurt.

Pit crews

Pit crews help make their team's vehicle work properly. During a **pit stop**, the pit crew have to work as a team to replace the tyres. A good pit crew can help their team to win a race.

DID YOU KNOW?

In **Formula 1**, all four tyres can be changed in less than three seconds!

24-hour racing

The famous Le Mans 24-Hour race takes place in Le Mans, France. Each car has a team of drivers, who swap around during the race. They race through the night.

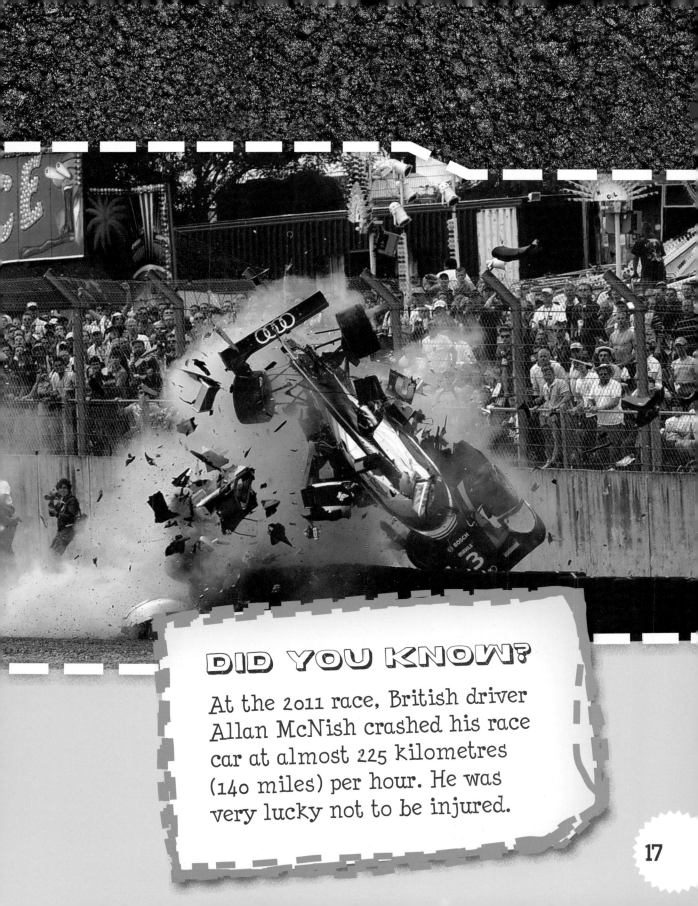

DID YOU KNOW?

At the 2011 race, British driver Allan McNish crashed his race car at almost 225 kilometres (140 miles) per hour. He was very lucky not to be injured.

Giant crowds

The Indianapolis 500 takes place every year at the Indianapolis Motor Speedway, in the United States. More than 400,000 people turn up to watch this race!

The Daytona 500 race attracts over 180,000 **spectators**.

DID YOU KNOW?

The Indianapolis Motor Speedway is also known as the "Brickyard". The **circuit** was originally built out of bricks!

The Race of Champions

The drivers compete in different vehicles to see who is the best.

At the end of every year, there is a spectacular event for all the world's best drivers. The Race of Champions takes place inside a sports stadium.

Sebastien Ogier won the Race of Champions on his first attempt.

DID YOU KNOW?

French rally star Sebastien Ogier won the 2011 Race of Champions.

Highest paid driver

The best drivers and riders in the world are very well paid. Two-time **Formula 1** world champion Fernando Alonso, who drives for Ferrari, is paid an incredible £23 million a year!

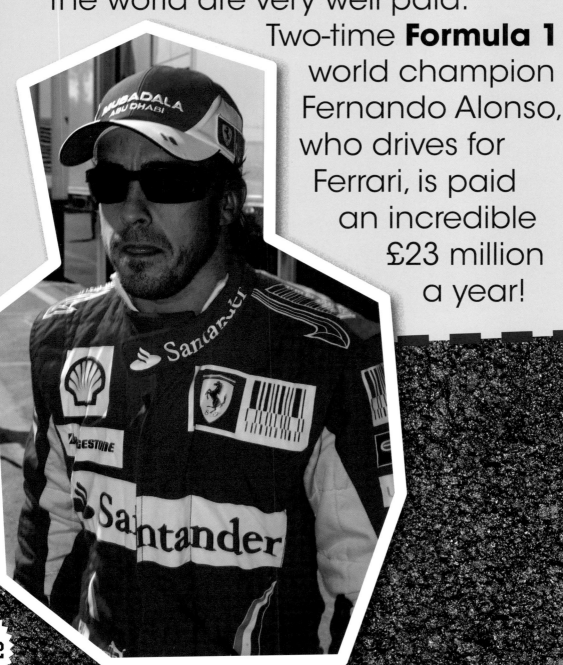

Great drivers

Sebastian Vettel won the **Formula 1** World Championship in 2010 and 2011. Vettel is the youngest driver ever to win a world championship. He started by racing **karts** when he was just seven years old.

RECORD BREAKERS

Michael Schumacher won a record 91 races in his Formula 1 career.

US driver Danica Patrick is the most successful female racer in the world. She started racing **karts** when she was 10 years old.

In 2008, Patrick became the first woman to win an **IndyCar** race.

RECORD BREAKERS

Superstar driver Jimmie Johnson won the **NASCAR** Sprint Cup Series championship five times in a row, which is an amazing record in the sport.

Quiz

Are you a superfan or a couch potato? Decide whether the statements below are true or false. Then look at the answers on page 31 and check your score on the fanometer.

1 Finnish driver Kimi Raikkonen has driven in **Formula 1, World Rally,** and **NASCAR.**

2 The fastest Formula 1 **pit crews** can change all four wheels in five seconds.

3 Lewis Hamilton is the youngest ever Formula 1 world champion.

TOP TIP
Some of the answers can be found in this book, but you may have to find some yourself.

4 Jimmie Johnson has won four NASCAR Sprint Cup Series championships.

5 Ferrari has won more Formula 1 races than any other team.

6 The top speed of a drag racing motorbike is 300 kilometres (186 miles) per hour.

FANOMETER

couch potato

allrounder

superfan

1   2   3   4   5   6

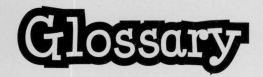

Glossary

accelerate speed up

circuit area built for car and bike racing. It includes the race track and the pits.

drag racing timed race over a short distance, usually a quarter of a mile

Formula 1 type of racing series. Formula 1 cars have an open cockpit and uncovered wheels.

IndyCar type of racing series in the United States. IndyCar cars have an open cockpit and uncovered wheels.

kart small four-wheeled vehicle used in racing

MotoGP type of racing series. This is the motorcycle version of Formula 1.

NASCAR type of racing series in the United States. NASCAR cars are like normal road cars, but much faster.

pit crews group of people who work as a team to make sure that the car is ready to race

pit stop when a car comes into the pits to have the tyres changed by the pit crew

spectators group of people who watch a game or show

Tyrrell Formula 1 team in the 1970s

World Rally also known as the World Rally Championship (WRC), this is a racing series. These cars do not race on circuits, but on public roads in timed stages.

Find out more

Books

Formula 1 (Motorsports), Clive Gifford (Franklin Watts, 2012)

Motorsports (Great Sporting Events), Clive Gifford (Franklin Watts, 2011)

Motorsports (Inside Sport), Clive Gifford (Wayland, 2012)

Website

f1forkidz.com
Find out more about the history of Formula 1 and check out photos of your favourite drivers in action.

Quiz answers

1) True.
2) False. It only takes the top teams about 3 seconds to change all four wheels (see page 15)!
3) False. Sebastian Vettel became the youngest ever Formula 1 world champion in 2010 (see page 24).
4) False. Johnson has won five NASCAR championships (see page 27).
5) True.
6) False, these bikes can go faster than 395 kilometres (245 miles) per hour (see page 7)!

Index